Martin Figura was born   ool in 1956. He joined the Army aged fifteen, leaving as a Major in 1997, after 25 years, to become a photographer, which is what he still is. He is currently doing an MA in Writing The Visual at Norwich School of Art and Design. He is a member of the performance group The Joy of Six, with whom he has performed across Britain and in New York.

He is the author of *This Man's Army*, a collection of photographs (Dewi Lewis Publishing), which contains a foreword by Billy Bragg and essays by Liz Wells and Anthony Beevor. He also wrote *The Little Book of Harm* (Firewater Press) which has been reprinted three times.

ahem

Martin Figura

Norwich

Egg Box Publishing
25 Brian Avenue, Norwich, NR1 2PH

The Egg Box Web Site Address is:
newwriting.net

The Joy of Six Web Site Address is:
joyofsix.co.uk

Martin Figura's Web Site Address is:
martinfigura.org.uk

First Published in Great Britain by
Egg Box Publishing, 2005

Copyright © Martin Figura, 2005

The author asserts the moral right to be
identified as the author of this work

ISBN 0-9543920-5-1

Printed and bound in Great Britain by
Biddles, King's Lynn

Designed by Alexander Gordon Smith

For Helen

For Sean

ahem...

9   I Wish

10   Ahem

12   Adrian Leaves the House at 7.30 on the Dot

13   Every Morning

14   The Amateur Photographer

15   The Competition

16   Death of an Amateur Photographer

17   Swaffham

18   Love Song

20   Wayne Rooney, Mona Lisa and the Crucifixion

21   Nighthawk

22   First Sight

23   An Angry Man

24   Fidelity

25   Enjambment

26   Diminishing Returns

27   Still Life

28   The Last Time

29   The Way It Is

30   Momentum

31   Male Standing Nude

32   A Dark Age

ahem...

33   The Dance

34   Blessed Virgin

35   In This Room

36   Poem Factory

37   Fighting in a Built-Up Area

38   One Wedding and a Divorce

39   Nursery Rhyme

40   Wind

41   Heart

42   Lollipops

43   Sean in San Francisco

44   Balsa Trees

45   3 Hillside Road, 1980

46   8 Lode Avenue, 2002

47   I'd Like to Say

48   Limpet Shell

49   Aunts

50   Christmas

51   Family Christmas

52   Fire

53   Rescue

54   Toothbrush

ahem...

55   School Trip

56   On the Road

57   Baby in a Playpen at the Glen Canyon Dam

58   Communing With Nature

60   Larder

61   I Work in the Arts Now

62   Would You Like Your Ears Done?

63   The Theft of the British Museum

64   Shopping and Flying

66   Poets' Retreat

69   Scholar

70   Luton Latin

71   A Party of Mythical Proportions

72   They Came From the Hills

77   Wise

78   Cars

79   (The Trouble With) Middle Aged People

80   A Paler Shade of Pop Music

81   Writing Group

82   Helen and Paris

83   New Dress

84   Looking Back

I wish

I had never
started
this poem

AHEM

After Ginsberg.

I saw the best suits of my parents' generation
        destroyed by poor tailoring, synthetic fibres
        and hysterical lapels,
dragging their shopping down the high streets
        of Albion in pacamacs with hairdos under
        hairnets and headscarves,
Brylcream-headed husbands burning pipe tobacco
        in walnut bowls and inhaling through
        the clenched teeth of repressed ardour,
who feared the wind rush in the negro streets
        of Victoriana blowing the sounds and smells
        that threaten the unfamiliar and didn't
        even know Elvis Presley existed yet,
who got drunk on home-made egg-flip at Christmas
        and sang the old songs around the piano
        while their kids were happy with a tangerine
        and dinky toy,
who saved so that one day they might have
        a little car and be saluted by the AA man
        as they drove by,
who were all the time boiling vegetables to eat with
        Spam while listening to the radiogram valves
        singing hot with Family Favourites and after sprouts
        there was Much Binding in The Marsh until
        Billy Cotton cried out WAKEY WAKEY and
        Bandstand glowed out in the deathly grey
        of cathode rays,

who on Fridays went dancing up the club in sixpence
    a week Montague Burton suits and crammed into
    eighteen hour girdles and mail order dresses with
    their blue hair piled on top, but just too soon to have
    been teenagers,
who tripped out to Skegness Vimto-fuelled in charabancs
    to shine under Billy Butlin's neon "our true intent is all
    for your delight" while being served brown ale by lasses
    from Doncaster in grass skirts under plastic palm trees
    in The Beachcomber Bar,
who never used the front room but kept it pure and the
    antimacassars pressed for visits by doctors or
    vicars or teachers for tinned salmon and tinned pears
    and tinned milk and always polished their front steps
    and never ran out of string,
who knew their place and never thought the universities
    were for the likes of them but prayed for office jobs
    for their children and stood for God Save The Queen
    at the Odeon and said how wonderful their policemen
    were and fought in the war for the likes of me,
who had more words for toilet than the Inuit have for snow
    and put their teeth in jars then slept in their vests
    under candlewick counterpanes in cold bedrooms
    with dreams of winning the pools and bungalows
    in Cheshire with inside loos and labour saving devices,
who at dawn trod into brown slippers onto cold brown
    linoleum and could only face the day through the
    sweet brown haze of a hundred cups of tea and
    twenty Capstan Full Strength.

Adrian Leaves the House
at 7.30 on the Dot

The moustache leaves the house first
Each twitching bristle gathering vital data
Air temperature
Pollen count
Moisture and
Barometric pressure
Transmitted to the extremities

The hand wrapped on the briefcase handle
The hand waving to the wife
The just kissed lips
The dormant penis tip
The right foot nudging at the day
Then the splayed bending left foot
That sets it all off
The whole see-sawing edifice
From the step
To the Ford Mondeo

Every Morning

she hauls her heavy self up from the bed,
delicious and fertile. He watches her stumble
to the bathroom where she glows in the light

of the frosted window. Sitting on the toilet
she stares at her toes which she raises as she pisses.
She feels for some Andrex and reaches it

between her legs. She stands up to the mirror,
turns the hot tap and puts her hand under it.
While she waits for the water she scoops

her hair back, then she bends to the sink
to splash her face. Her vertebrae
rise up to be counted.

The Amateur Photographer

She has grown to hate the sun.
The sun that lights up the world;
creates miracles of ordinary objects;
draws patterns on holiday sands that
send Roger running for his camera.

Of course these holiday sands
are not the flat smooth sort you can lie on,
soak up the sun on, read your book on. No
these sands have been whipped into ridges
by North Sea winds that turn a wind-break

into a kite. Her holidays have long been spent
huddled on a rock miles from the nearest
café or bar while Roger crouches over his tripod
waiting for the light. *This is beauty* he says
man and nature. Who wants to lie around
with all those boring sun-seekers?

I do, she thinks, I do.

Competition

She must sit through it. Two hours
of slides, pretty much the same
as last month and the month before.

Then another couple of hours
in the pub discussing f-stops, film
speeds and bitching about the winner.

Occasionally Roger remembers
she's there and asks
Are you alright, my little gadget bag?

Next month's theme is 'moods'.
I could do that for him she thinks.
I could show him a fucking mood.

Death of an Amateur Photographer

She must stand there
On the third
In her red anorak

Try and look like you're enjoying yourself for Christ's sake Julie

She smiles
He lines it up
It must be just right
He backs up a little
He thinks he should buy a wide-angle lens
He backs up a little more
She watches him near the edge
Her smile becomes more convincing
His heels rock over
The balance tips
In favour of gravity
His arms windmill
The camera is hurled
His face panics
His eyes plead
She waves
He's gone

Swaffham

We stole into Swaffham in the dead
of the windiest night of the year
and hijacked the wind turbines.
Once aboard we turned the controls

to full. The dials all hurtled to red:
alarms cried out,
blades blurred,
and the turbines began to shake.

We rose into the night, tearing Swaffham
right out of the ground. Whooping for joy
we swung our great vessel out west
across the country, scattering sprouts

along the way. We crossed the mountains
of Wales and Ireland and lurched away
over the deep Atlantic, steering by stars.
We kept cover by eluding one dawn

and chasing another. It seemed an
age before our tired and huddled mass
sighted the Statue of Liberty and knocked
the torch clean out of her hand. It took

all our skill to steer down the East River
and out over the Upper East Side, to settle
in Central Park. Then as new day shadows
of Fifth Avenue apartment blocks

fingered their way across the Market Place
and shops, Bill Turnbull drew his curtains
and called out to Ethel to come
and look at this.

Love Song

After Betjeman.

Miss J. Cooper Clark, Miss J. Cooper Clark,
Wizened and dampened in the afternoon dark,
What digestive biscuits we dunked in our tea,
Steaming and dripping in the caff – you and me!

Love up the alley, love in the park, I'm your boy
And o when you swallow, sweetness of joy.
With careless morals on white high heels you embark,
I am weak from your loveliness, Joan Cooper Clark.

Miss Joan Cooper Clark, Miss Joan Cooper Clark,
You're dead mad you are, I bet y'can bark.
My hands are cold inside her dress,
But my peroxide-headed bird, she loves me no less.

Her father's emphysema wheezes from the chair,
As we swing past the parlour, and sneak up the stairs.
Sex 'not-protected' and a glimpse of her bits untanned,
Oh! nicotine-stained-nail-biting-girl's hand.

The stench of the toilet, sound of the sirens,
The view of Joanee's laddered nylons,
As I fumble with button flies,
Things are struggling, romance-wise.

On the floor of her bedroom lie dog-ends and shoes,
And the wood-chipped walls are be-stuck with used tissues
And festering, questioning settles the skidmark
On the Poundstretcher knickers of Joan Cooper Clark.

Miss J. Cooper Clark, Miss J. Cooper Clark,
Yer hairdo is a local landmark.
O! Salford twilight on the Manchester Ship Canal!
O! Rusholme's fabulous femme fatale!

And the scent of morning sickness, and the periods missed,
And her ominous, ominous father, angry and pissed.
We sat in the pub, the choices were stark
And now I'm engaged to Miss Joan Cooper Clark.

Wayne Rooney, Mona Lisa
and the Crucifixion

To be worshipped is to die. It is the only thing
we can be clear about. The rest is lost to myth.
Can I even remember why I was smiling? The
softness of my beautiful eyes may explain it and
the satisfaction of knowing Leonardo passed over
noblemen for three years to paint me.

This was before adoration became tiresome; some kind
of crucifixion, the public sacrifice of self. What is said
now, blurs so easily at the edges; loses its meaning
in the cacophony. The slight parting of my lips is
perhaps no longer for the purposes of enigma and allure
but for the need to be understood. I may be about to speak.

At any moment, through that bullet proof glass screen
I might clearly be seen mouthing the words fuck off.

Nighthawk

If only Hopper were still around
to paint this scene of me
at home alone on Saturday night,
it might look as if I'd at least been
somewhere interesting.

There would be a streetlight
right outside the window
to pick me out against the
muted colours of the room.
There would be a lot of green.

The empty wine bottle, the
drapes. You wouldn't be able
to tell that it was the TV
I was contemplating, or that
those ochre flecks on my chest

were dry Sugar Puffs that didn't
make it into my mouth from the bowl
and are now stuck to my shirt.

First Sight

You don't know me
but I sat next to you
on the bus once.

I got your name off your bag
and your number from the book.
I would ring, just to hear your voice.

When you changed your number
I started watching you
and got to know your little ways.

By my observations and notes
on your habits I have worked out
exactly what you want.

So when you get home tonight
I will be waiting there for you.
There's no need to worry
I'll tell you what to do.

An Angry Man

He banished love from the house
like you would a working dog.

If he was not asleep, then
he was angry. Now there is

only himself to be angry with.
That and the television.

Fidelity

He lets his relation
ships over
lap. Never finish

ing with one wo
man until he has an
other one, safe

ly in tow. The wo
men regard this as de
spicable and pro

test. He def
ends him
self by say

ing that as a po
et, sure
ly he's entit

led to a little en
jambment.

En
Jam
Bment

With Helen Ivory

Straw
Berry
Rasp
Berry
Black
Currant
Dam
Son
Goose
Berry
Mar
Malade
Plum

Diminishing Returns

I said I loved you
You said I
Know

I said can we make love
You said not
Now

I said do you love me
You said
No

I said
O

Still Life

After Sarah Lynch – Untitled 2, 2002 from Suspended Reality.

They are barely still, it would only take
the slightest breeze for their commitment
to the genre to waiver. How they got up there
in the first place, is a wonder. The whole contraption
is hanging by a thread. And yet it seems poised
to set off on some tentative journey; dragging
its moorings behind. How far could it possibly get
on those five spindle legs without toppling? In any case
it wouldn't take much in the way of malevolence
to bring it down. One snip or a nudge should do.

The Last Time

I don't remember the last time
we made love and it troubles me.
Of course at the time, I didn't know
it was the last time, or perhaps
I would have made more of an effort.
Paid attention to the details, tried
something different; spectacular even.
But as far as I was concerned it was just
another ride on the merry-go-round.
I guess that's the way it usually happens.

The Way It Is

So here you are on my doorstep
clutching at stalks: garage forecourt
flowers with a two-ninety-nine day-glo
sticker, a bottle of wine from the One
Stop Shop.

You hand over this common currency
with a few whispered words of love
that bear all the hallmarks of a shop
bought card.

By the look on your face
you're expecting some kind
of reward.

You'd better come in then.

Momentum

I live

        my life

like

        a drunk

    on stilts

as long

      as I

maintain

        momentum

   everything

      will be

  alright

    Sooner

        or later

though

   I'm going to get tired

      and that's hard

    ground down

    there

Male Standing Nude

In my head I thought I knew what I looked like naked.
Standing here in front of the mirror with nothing
on it is clear that I don't. I often see myself
naked, you can't help it when there
is a mirror and you're changing.
As the years go by you stop
looking and just glance
while sucking your
stomach in. The
idea of others
seeing you
naked and
gazing at
your
cock
is when
things get
relative size-wise.
It's denied of course
but if this was not a poem
but a picture then you would
not start looking from the top would
you; man or woman. This is not vanity
or the delusion that everyone can't wait to see
my delicious cock. I know that it's just curiosity
and re-assurance for the men (we are all shaken since
slow-motion replays of Linford Christie came to our screens)
but it makes you think, doesn't it? Of course, this is just a poem

I could tell you anything.

A Dark Age

After Cornelia Parker.

This explosion is the dying of the universe.
The bright centre of it hurling all its matter
ever so slowly against the invisible edge.
Stuff and time bent out of shape.

Lately it has begun to accelerate. You can
see it in the weather. The blame seems to lie
with the man in his shed. Given that time
is running out, he is experimenting in the dust

amongst the nuts and bolts; searching
for a parallel universe. Another dimension
through hyperspace, to where we might travel
and carefully put ourselves back together.

The Dance

These three rough stones have fallen from heaven.
A pyramid of dimpled flesh; simple peasant women
not given to grace or the company of gods. At this
ritual transformation: they smooth each other's edges
with rasping emery boards, comb and tease their
tangled hair into ribbons. They put on powder masks,
paint lips warning red and draw black around those
watching eyes. Soon they'll fasten up stocking tops
and put on party dresses.

Now in glorious high shoes they can shine down
the dirt road to the village square. The late sun turns
the dust to flame and them to gardens of bright flowers.
The tables are set around the Fountain of Venus and
there are honey cakes to eat. As the night falls violins
and Spanish guitars start a gentle seduction, before the Latin
rhythm takes hold and the dancing must begin. Mercury
is posed under lanterns; orbs that hang down from the stars.

He turns his face up to them as if to the heavens. In return
he is illuminated; made innocent and beautiful in this pure
light. Any of our three Graces would desire the burn
of Cupid's arrow to seek for them such a lover. But then
a shiver runs through the almond trees where Zephyr waits,
returned from the olive groves, sun-dark skin glistening sweat
in the moon's light. He moves towards them and their disguises
fall away. They are barefoot in a pool of lipstick. The flowers
of their dresses release their thick perfume.

Blessed Virgin

Just boys and monks;
no girls in this universe.

That was until Mary from the village
found us in our den
in the out of bounds wood
and kissed us one by one.

After that, we went down there
all we could and Mary did her stuff.
Our gang grew larger, until the night
we heard the unmistakable sound
of monks moving through the trees.

Then came spanking,
letters to parents,
Sermons.

But still at night,
under the sheets,
activity continued.

In This Room

In this room I work
Table, four chairs on a dark wood floor
Monochrome photographs on white walls
Green pottery on a shelf
A garden through open doors

In this room I work
Do my accounts
Send and receive messages
Make calls
Edit pictures
And in sporadic bursts of displacement
Write the occasional poem

Poem Factory

It looks as if there is nothing here, nothing more
than converging lines leading you to burnt-out windows.
But you have to negotiate those pillars hanging down red
and the yellow has to find its place in the conversation.
From this perspective the colours echo, sometimes loud,
other times so you can hardly hear them. These structures
hold it all together. In the space between there are tyre marks
and white lines; ghosts from when they built army trucks here.
Outside the frame there is the noise and diesel smell of the past:
of men preparing trucks to carry other men, then sending them off.
The right hand edge of the page gently reflects this all back.
I don't need to tell you that it's about to be ripped down.

Fighting in a Built-Up Area

The road is full of holes.
The door is hanging off.
The walls have crumbled
under mortar fire
and the windows
are all shot out.

The questions are loaded.
Every glance is booby-trapped.
Each gesture is a trip wire.

There's a sniper
in the lounge.

One Wedding and a Divorce

After Auden.

Pack up my stuff, scream down the hall,
You scheming bitch I can't take any more,
Banish the good times, let damage be done,
Bring out the hire van, let the solicitors come.

Let your friends and relations pick over my bones,
Put my memory in a sack and fill it with stones,
Cut my image out of the wedding photos,
Throw it in brambles, where nothing else grows.

She was my pain, my heart, my darkness and hell,
My reason for working on Sundays as well,
My reminder of failure, my executioner's song;
Whatever I tried to do, it was always wrong.

The vows that we took, are broken each one;
Put away your spells, the magic has gone,
Put up the shutters, close up for good,
Give up on giving, turn into wood.

Nursery Rhyme

She's as cute as cherry pie
The apple of her daddy's eye
Mom's in bud with number two
Their Disney dreams are coming true

But the son who came along
Was not quite right, a little wrong
And why he was out of place
Was written on his little face

He'd never make President
This little bundle heaven sent
Anyone with eyes could see
For them the dream was not to be

On the screen the doctor shows
How to make it so no one knows
And what their kind of money buys
A little mongol boy's disguise

~

Take a face that didn't fit
Then cut it up a little bit
Squander his identity
A tribute to your vanity

Wind

Amy fitted in the crook of my arm.
Her mouth stretched round my fingertip.
She had colic for nearly three years.
Her stomach rock hard, she would scream.

One day, when she'd been crying all day
we called out the doctor.
He came and stood in the door
and said it was only wind.

We said we were worried and thought
it was something more serious.
He said it wasn't and he hadn't been home
since eight that morning.

I wish I'd said something to him,
or even hit him. But I was young
and tired. Twenty years later
I'm still rehearsing a response.

Heart

Her skin was wet and so tight
it looked as if it might split.
Her mouth gasping,
her eyes wide open and on us.
Five more times we watched her
drift through swing doors.

He found us sitting on the step
and told us not to worry
we were good people.
He had held her heart in his hand
and it was working fine. I pictured it
pulsing on his latex glove, her blood
dribbling purple through his fingers.

Lollipops

They phone all the time
Is Sean in?
The other night
Two turned up at the door
Angel faces
Sucking lollipops

It doesn't seem fair to me
That it comes so easily to him
On the other hand
I wouldn't want the girls
With lollipops to stop calling

Sean in San Fransisco

Blading in the park above the wharves
On his K 2 2 50s
Wraparound Raybans
Bought that day at Crossroads on Market
Hair gelled
Baggies hanging off his scraggy arse
Blue T-shirt
Billowed by the air conditioned breeze
He was looking pretty cool
Behind him
Pacific Heights
Before him
The edge of the world

Balsa Trees

They shoot up and gangle like teenage boys, but abhor
hanging around in clumps. They put themselves
about the jungle, sheltering their slow neighbours
from the sun with their protecting hood of leaves.

The Balsa Trees are dying by the time those
they care for are strong enough to cope. With a
broad Spanish axe one native will let these heroes
fall to the forest floor, then carry them to the river.

Balsa is the Spanish word for raft. Kiln dried it can
carry four times its own weight and absorb shock.
Scalpelled into an aeroplane (it is almost lighter than
air) and with the merest engine it can fly like a hawk.

Now it can really take to the skies,
its shadow racing over trees.

3 Hillside Road, 1980

From a sunny honeymoon to ice
on the windows and water frozen
in the cistern. A storage heater
takes up half the living room
and a week's pay just to get it warm.
Psychedelic upholstery and curtains
set against magnolia walls. In the lino-floored
kitchen I cook the first meal, curried bacon
and beans. The square army furniture
swallows wedding presents. We put
ornaments out with a sense of adventure.

This house is ours.

8 Lode Avenue, 2002

You are still beautiful
I was never handsome
Rainwater from a blocked gutter
Crashes onto the stone path
Inside only traces remain
Stains and marks
Testimony to clumsiness

This house is for sale

I'd Like To Say

Twenty five years resolved
by a piece of paper. It hardly
seems to do it justice. Shouldn't
there be more of a fuss?

I'd like to say it was all my fault.
I'd like to think that I'm a kind man,
just not your kind of man, anymore.
That's not to say that your kind of man
isn't kind.

I'd like to say that you remain the only girl in the world.
I'd like to say that those last years were as good as the first.
I'd like to say I still love you, just not in that way.
I'd like to say all this to your face,

but I've written it down to make sure
I get to say everything I want to say.
You might say how is that different?
I might say that's not fair.
Then we would be right back
where we were.

Limpet Shell

A sharp hooked dental tool
driven hard into the black heart
of a tooth, until it catches

on a ledge. Then the tooth
dragged inside out from a howling mouth
into the shape of a conical hat.

Inside it nicotine and coffee stains
caramelise with the grey filling.
The old inside outside now

aching to be rubbed smooth.

Aunts

Like the riders of the Apocalypse, there are
four of them. These are soldier aunts advancing
down your path. It is a wonder they can move, given
the weight of their concerns, but their scarves must hurry
to keep up. With so little time left they have decided
to devote their remaining years to disapproval.

They occupy your sofa,
straight-backed and Kevlar-haired.
Knees accuse you.
Ears have heard it all before.
Eyes see through any argument.
Noses sniff out fecklessness.
And their tongues,

their tongues
can take your head
clean off.

Christmas

He's really fucked up this time
He's let down everyone
He's back home with Mum and Dad

His job's gone
He's thirty seven

She's got the kids and the upper hand
Given what he's done
She's not about to make it easy

He curls up in an armchair with his football annual
If he could, he'd crawl right back in the womb

Rescue

You find each other
in the dark
and cling together.

She makes everything better
and you do
the same for her.

Only she knows
when you're healed
you'll go.

It's happened before.
You're so sure
she's wrong.

She says
it's alright,
that's the way it is.

When you do go
you try to do it kindly,
but you're selfish and inept.

Then you feel bad
and try to make it right.
But it just gets crueller.

I suppose she will carry on
without expectation
and without you,

now you're rescued.

Toothbrush

He just wandered in with a Daily Mirror
tucked under his arm and our milk
in the other hand. We didn't know
quite what to say as he put the kettle on
and made us all tea. He seemed to know
our requirements, milk no sugar for me
and one sugar and milk for you. Oblivious
to our raised eyebrows, he settled down
in my armchair and switched on the TV.

I still can't believe we didn't just ask him
to leave, but if you don't act immediately
in these circumstances, then it becomes awkward.
It was when he used my toothbrush that I thought
enough was enough, that and his lack of pyjamas
as he swung past on his way to the spare room.
But you said 'Leave it, let's see what happens.
He'll probably be off in the morning.' So
I let it go, but that's me all over.

Slowly but surely I was usurped. That's
my cardigan he's wearing right now. It fits
him better than it ever fitted me. The kids
took to him straight away. He can fix bikes,
do magic tricks and homework. The Cat
ignores him and not me. Every evening
you all get together on the sofa and decide
what to watch. It is as if I am invisible.

But I know that I'm not
because you all lift your feet
while I'm hoovering.

School Trip

We were struck below the waterline
The fibreglass cracked wide and ragged
The Shropshire Union Canal slipping in

Mr O'Mara stood calm and firm
One foot on the towpath, one on the barge
Pulling out boys and girls hand over hand

'Come on now Sister Clare, quickly'
Sister Clare grasped the helm
'I can't, I signed for the boat'

Mr O'Mara summoned all the angels
Called upon Jesus, Mary and Joseph
But Sister Clare was going down with the ship

Mr O'Mara despaired of nuns
'Heavens above Clare it's not the bloody Titanic'
Sister Clare began to sing *Just a closer walk with thee*

The bow rose and the stern eased back
Sister Clare's habit billowed around her flushed face
Making of her an immense black water lily

On the Road

A near-death experience in the blizzard of 2003.

this isn't a long road but it's taking a long time getting there a little weather comes our way and day passes into night and into day again but i'm ok smug and snug as a bug in my heated seat seven miles in seven hours isn't so bad when there are good tunes on the radio and the taillights glow and the snow on the ground shines in my headlights and my tyres grip then it just goes dark and quiet and cold my car has had enough just like that at 2am still i just roll a cigarette get the transistor radio from my bag and call the rescue man 9 o'clock he says so i settle down wrap the sleeping bag around and roll another cigarette then there's a face at the window it could've been the angel of death but when i buzzed the window down it was bill the trucker we pushed the lazy car off to the side and he went on his way i crawled back in and tried to buzz the window up again but it didn't want to go it was just too tired so the snow saw its chance and drifted onto me and the passenger seat it could all end here six miles east of stevenage listening to janice long on radio 2 revelling in all the callers she was getting it must have seemed like she was back in her glory days on saturday night radio 1 i prayed to my god and every other god promised to be good and all sorts of stuff until they let the window crawl its way back up and i rolled another cigarette and started to think about all the promises i couldn't possibly live up to and waited to be rescued.

Baby in a Playpen at the
Glen Canyon Dam

After Joel Sternfeld.

You do understand
that you cannot contain nature,
indefinitely?

Sooner or later
it will have its way,
so is there any point

in trying to stop it?
It will already be pushing
against its boundaries.

Sure, it looks calm now,
but given time, it could:
sweep away landscapes,

rip through villages,
hurl trees down the high street for fun,
take your car for a spin.

Communing With Nature

Sitting on a log looking at the wonder of it all
I need a cigarette
Roll it neat
Spark it up
Take it down deep to do its work
Cough it up stale

The crows answer back
So we get to talking
Hacking back and forth at each other about stuff
You know
The war and that
Which roadkills taste best
How long they need to be left before you tuck in

I say I've never talked to crows before
They say that's the trouble
No one ever does
People hear our voice all right
But no one really listens
Nothing changes
I tell them I'll listen
And do

So I hear about how tough it is to be a crow
In a world of graceful songbirds
What it means to have an awkward walk to be mocked
To be assumed to like jazz

How many people take them for rooks or ravens
Jays even
I mean
Jesus one says
Do I even look remotely like a motherfucking jay?

Then there's the whole symbol of death thing
Try living with that
You can't fly near any sensitive artistic types
Without scaring them shitless
One guy even cut off his ear

I say I understand
They say I can't
But thank me for listening

Larder

In the event
of rationing
she would be alright

for quite some time.
Then she will
be enjoying jelly,

while those around
will have to make do
with less tasty puddings.

There are other treats too,
in the surprise
of those tins

that have lost
identity; their labels
faded away.

Who knows
what they'll
come out with.

I Work in the Arts Now

I meet creative people
Nice people
Sensitive people

Sometimes they ask me
How long have I been a photographer
And when I tell them four years
They ask me what I did before
That's when I tell them

I was in the Army
They usually look puzzled then
Shocked even and seek reassurance

How long for, they ask
Hoping it was a brief and hateful experience
Twenty five years, I say
They're starting to get worried

They hardly dare ask what I did
But they do
That's when I tell them
I was an accountant

Now they do look puzzled
As if they can't decide
Which is the most appalling
Piece of information

The soldiering or
The accountancy

Would You Like Your Ears Done?

It was only when he set about them
with his clippers, that I realised
what he meant. Apparently ears also
carry eyebrow consent. With my head
still buzzing I stumbled from the chair
clutching a complimentary tissue, over-
tipped, got out of there.

By the time I reached the avenue
my leather coat was tweed, my trainers
highly polished brogues, corduroy
replaced my jeans. A regimental tie
was grasping at my throat. A battered hat
snagged with fish-flies, perched there
on my head.

A Telegraph I don't remember buying
was in the basket of the bicycle I didn't
know I had. The take-away on the corner
took me back to Singapore. A dead heading
neighbour called out 'Good morning Major'.
It was only when I waved my hand I saw
the liver spots.

There was a woman in the kitchen in a pinny
making jam. I said 'Who the devil are you?'
She said 'My name is Marjorie, we've been married
fifty years.' I took this information down the hallway
to the lounge, where I reached for my tobacco
at exactly the same time as the old man in the mirror
who was looking back at me.

The Theft of the British Museum

Only the moon was watching as the black
Ford Transit van slipped into Bloomsbury
and cut its lights. The thieves worked fast,
but carefully; if they were to get it all in
they could not afford wasted space
around the wheel arches.

Months of meticulous planning paid off
and they had the building smartly packed
in the back of the van well before dawn.
The pillars, disguised as carpets, went
on the roof-rack. Red rags hung off
either end. They didn't want to blow the job

for the sake of a minor traffic violation.
The engine started first time. This was
a Transit LWB 3-5-0 EL Jumbo, as capable
as any in its class. It grunted and sparked
down Museum Street and into the night
avoiding speed bumps, leaving a mammoth

white elephant stall. The history of the world
crammed between Montague Place
and Russell Street. Bronze heads
from the Kingdom of Benin rubbed
against stone Roman noses. Empire
leant against empire, age against age.

Shopping and Flying

On the way to the bus
I just decided to do it
Rode up on to the balls of my feet
And continued upwards

I have no idea where the urge came from
I have no particular history on this
No overwhelming interest
In the mechanics or science of it
No romantic notions on what it must be like to be a bird
But here I was
Hovering above the cul de sac
Wishing I had brought a camera

The village soon behind me
I cavorted for a while with the seagulls at Milton tip
While people below fed the hungry hole
With the remains of previous shopping trips

High up over Chesterton
I watched the cars dribble up the hardening arteries
Into the city's heart
To be pumped out rich with the oxygen of stuff

Then I swooped out of the sun
Down to the river
Biffing punting tourists into the Cam
Gathering exclamations:

Mon Dieu!
Achtung!
Bollocks!
Merde!
Bastardo!

When I ran out of victims
I caught a thermal out over Cherry Hinton
To astonish the golfers of Gog Magog
Pocketing balls in mid air

Leaving Pringle sweaters filled with desolation
I headed into town
Slipping the underpants
(That I happened to have in my pocket) over my trousers
I addressed the flabbergasted down below:
'I'm terribly sorry I can't stop to chat
I have a universe to save'

Poets' Retreat

Cottage Yorkshire Dales *Sleeps twelve, remote and ideal for writing retreats. Tel: 01980 666666*

Sitting by the fire whittling, I wait for Cerberus
to tell me they're here. Cerberus can smell poet,
it's the wet corduroy. He barks three times
before they've reached the gate.

I open the door just as they go for the bell.
Tha'll be the poets then.
Tha'll be sticking t' path.
They said they would.
It'll be a cold day in hell.

It's a good mile to the cottage.
The path is harsh and they wince
as the weather comes at them.
They are thrilled. Their heads'
are full of the imagery of it.
They can't wait to get it down on paper.

They're from Cambridge, pasty-faced academic
types. They should be easy meat. Not as easy
as the metaphysicals though. They hadn't even
been sure they were here until it was too late.

Then, full of their own cleverness, there was
the Movement Poets. Well, they're not moving now.
And as for the bloody romantics, they were so fey
and fragile the weather got them first.

The Liverpudlians and African-Caribbeans
may be streetwise, but let me tell you
there are no streets here and they died
crying for their mothers in each others' arms.

The Ted Hughes workshop was the best
sport. Eleven poets lured to a slow death
with a single dead rabbit. A taste of their
own medicine; fresh pickings for the crows.

The language poets tried to explain themselves
but I had no idea what they were on about and
to be frank, I didn't care. But I think they understood
me when I said: sorry I and am me you irri
tate must so I you s l o w l y k i l l

Only Craig Raine got away. He's quicker
than he looks and I just winged him. He went
scurrying and wailing into the hills. I was
after him, but he blocked the gate with a copy

of his Collected Poems: nineteen-seventy-eight
to nineteen-ninety-eight. Now he roams the moors
worrying sheep. Sightings are part of local legend.
A hairy beast in tattered Y fronts, roaring and stumbling
through the woods looking for his glasses.

The concrete poets, for obvious reasons, were less quick
and paid the price. But they have found a certain peace
and are with their own kind holding up the flyover
at the Junction with the A66.

The Poet Laureate came to fish in the very river
I disposed of Stevie Smith in. Her arm is still
sticking out, very much drowned, definitely not
waving. I've jammed his head in a dry stone wall
as a warning to others, a ball of paper stuffed
in his mouth. His final work – unfinished:

I don't know about you
I can only speak for me
But I really enjoyed
The Queen's Golden Jubilee

I quite like it when they run for it, Cerberus
and I refer to it as 'The Emily Dickinson fifty-
metre-dash!' We are in the chariot – right on
their tails. Back at the cottage the Cambridge lot
are unpacking, laying out their towels, while
somewhere in the distance, something or other
howls.

Scholar

It would be nice to be a scholarly poet.
The sort who can seamlessly introduce French
into a poem,
à la baisse d'un chapeau[1],
as it were.

I suspect that if
I were to attempt such a thing
I would *chute sur mon cul*[2],
thus making my ignorance
more apparent.

[1] At the drop of a hat
[2] Fall on my arse

Luton Latin

Inno
Innis
Innit

A Party of Mythical Proportions

Helen was busy in the kitchen. She estimated,
given the numbers, that she would need to make
about a thousand chips. Meanwhile Pyrrhus
was in the garden with a petrol can and matches
sparking up the barbeque, while Jason greeted
guests in his new yellow fleece that he got
from Argos. Cassandra had tried to warn them
that if they put Bacchus in charge of the bar
then things were bound to get out of hand.

'Well, who'd have thought it?' Prometheus said later
after his innocent young brother had let Pandora
get him into the spare room, where he eagerly opened
her box. Eurydice was already dead to the world
by this time, leaving Orpheus in his underpants, singing
his head off. Zeus had spiked Cronus's drink, who promptly
threw up on his children and was trying to clean them up
with Ajax. Harry Adne had, by then, completely lost the thread
and only wanted to go home, but couldn't find his way out.

Mars had started to get arsey with the Trojans; telling them to get on
their so called house-warming present and piss off. But there were
increasingly more of them than him and even Cyclops could see
things were going to get ugly. Oedipus had began to wish
he'd accepted his mother's offer of an early night. It was then that
Styx began to make everyone cocktails, using plenty of ice.

They Came From the Hills

Ancient Egypt

They came from the hills
The scribes of Ancient Egypt
Crossing deserts
Fearing not Ammut
Or Sobek
And paying little heed to Hathor
By the Nile they wrote
With calamus on papyrus
On the farms
And in the workshops
They brought order to the deities of Hermopolis

And to the Pharaohs

Taxes and the knowledge of
How many bricks it takes to build a pyramid

Mesopotamia

There in the Fertile Crescent
Between the Euphrates and the Tigris
The counting men came down
To the valleys of Mesopotamia
To number the years

To the Sumerians
Then to the Assyrians
From Ninevah to Babylon
Where King Hammurabi
Etched his law
On black basalt

An eye for an eye
A tooth for a tooth
The first balance sheet

Ancient Greece

Sent by the gods of Olympus
To the sea and Athenian temples
These men of numbers
Counted votes and carved disbursements
Onto marble stones which lay inside
The neat columns of the Parthenon
Until Lord Elgin came

But no Barbarian at the gate could plunder
That knowledge of truth and justice and existence
Laid there by the great philosophers
Aristotle
Plato
Socrates
And Dimitri from accounts

Renaissance Italy

Frater Luca Bartolomes Pacioli

He came north from Tuscany
This renaissance man
Over the hills
To the glacial lakes
And Sulphur springs
Of Lombardia
Where the artists saw
The beauty of equilibrium

There in the shadows of The Alps
He wrote of double entry book-keeping
And Leonardo drew
To see to it
That credit was given
Where credit was due

Divina Proportione

A world of harmony and balance
Where all men knew
Not only the value of everything
But the cost of it too

London

They come now from
The Chilterns
The Cotswolds
The South Downs
And Highgate Hill
Pale men with soft hands
Chalk striped and laptop laden

They emerge from the ground
And from over the river
To streets by City Wall
Throgmorton,
Lombard
And Threadneedle

There amongst the Merchant Halls
In the towers
And at the tables
A day of reckoning begins.

Wise

You go through life making mistakes and learning. When you're young you do this with zeal and enthusiasm, knowing one day the sum of the parts of your knowledge will amount to wisdom.

Then when you speak, it will be with a quiet authority. People will be drawn to you to resolve their problems. Encouraged you will apply yourself to the big questions and put the world to rights.

Then one morning you wake and ache a little. All you want is a comfy chair. Other people's problems bore you. Your head is stuffed with conflicting facts, making it impossible to draw conclusions.

If at some point you did reach a critical mass of knowledge when everything fell into place and made sense, you must have slept through it.

Cars

His cars were always Volvos.
Sturdy and reliable, built to work
around the clock. Neither aerodynamic
nor exciting, but prepared to accept
a lot of baggage. Then

after nearly forty years
and three Volvos, he bought
a bright red sports car.

A few short months later
he lost control
on a dangerous curve.

They found him
smiling in a ditch.

(The Trouble With) Middle Aged People

Middle aged people today don't know they're born.
What do they think they're up to?
They should be occupying their time with:

> jigsaws,
>
> the litter problem,
>
> gravy,
>
> coach trips to the Norfolk Lavender Fields.

But no, they're at Glastonbury
boring the arse off young people
about Dylan or how they saw The Who
in their hey day in 68, doing degrees
with no possible practical application,
motorcycling across India to find themselves.

There's even one reading you this poem, and look
he's wearing red trainers with white stripes.

A Paler Shade of Pop Music

Pop music today is so meaningless
How can young people relate to it
They will never *scaramouche scaramouche*
Let alone *skip the light fandango*

Writing Group

When my turn comes,
the words fall like lead from my lips
and drag their sorry arses across the parquet floor,
to my fellow poets.

A period of shoe gazing ensues.

At last Andrea offers
'It's very atmospheric.'
Like a fart, Wayne thinks.
But outwardly they cling to the remark
like drowning men to the wreckage,
with murmurs and nods.

More silence.

Then, as ever, Peter opens the batting.
He's not sure about the ending,
which turns out to be
what everyone else was thinking.

Confident now, Anne
casts doubt on the beginning.
No one disagrees.

Finally, André thinks I could
'Probably lose the middle section.'

Thank you I say, that was really useful.

Helen and Paris

Dancing barefoot in a vivid pink dress
with the Arc de Triomphe behind you.
You have a rose between your teeth.

I'm snapping away in the fashion
of a photographer from the sixties.
Passers-by are hit by the flash blur.

You are the only colour in the picture.

New Dress

While I was away
you have bought
this fabulous blue dress.
A floral print in the style
of the forties.

You're not sure and ask
what it says about you.

I say you look
like your husband
is away at the front
and you miss him.

You pin the cleavage up a bit.
You don't want to seem that lonely.

Looking Back

Dead to the world, he didn't notice the dirt
rattle onto the lid of his coffin. Therefore
he was not upset that no one wept or hurt

when his head emptied out onto the floor
and the only emotion he induced was revulsion.
The policeman with the megaphone was more

nervous than he was. To think that badminton
could put that much colour in a woman's face
was sheer naivety. At the wedding her eyes shone

for him, like semi-precious stones through fine lace.
She walked into the room and changed his life. What
his mother found him doing was, she said, a disgrace.

The school reports he brought home were not
as good as his sister's. He was only ever a thorn
in their side. He hadn't hit the parent jackpot.

From the very beginning they always looked careworn.
When the man in a green mask and coat struck the first blow
he began to wish he hadn't been born.

ACKNOWLEDGMENTS

Martin Figura would like to thank the following for all their
help and support

Helen Ivory, Emily and Lizzy Dening, Sarah Blomfield, Andrea Porter,
Anne Berkeley, George Szirtes, Peter Howard, André Mangeot, Michelle
Remblance, Matt Harvey, Wayne Hill, Tom Sherin and Dodie Carter,
First Tuesday, Caféwriters, One Night Stanza
and of course Gordon Smith at Egg Box.

A version of Ahem was previously published in *The Rialto*.
A version of I Work in the Arts Now was previously published in
Smith's Knoll and *East Life*
Family Christmas was published in *Rattapallax* (USA)
Married, I Work in the Arts Now, Adrian Leaves the House at 7.30 on the
Dot and Family Christmas were previously published in
the Joy of Six's *Flirtation*.

Aisle16

Live From the Hellfire Club

'Poetry has come of age.'
The Guardian

'They do with words what
I try to do with art.'
Ralph Steadman

newwriting.net

André Mangeot

Mixer

'His eye is acute – for poetry,
violence, the cruelties of love …
his poetry shakes the ground, as
only good poetry does.'
R. V. Bailey

n e w w r i t i n g . n e t

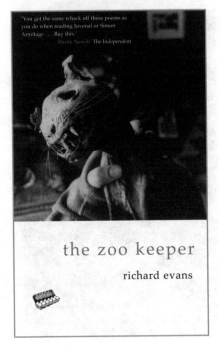

'You get the same whack off these poems as you do when reading Juvenal or Simon Armitage . . . Buy this.'
Martin Newell: The Independent

the zoo keeper

richard evans

Richard Evans

The Zoo Keeper

'Poetry as it should be, red in
tooth and claw.'
Concrete

'Buy this.'
Martin Newell, The Independent

newwriting.net

COME WHAT YOU

WISHED FOR

 Ramona Herdman

Ramona Herdman
Come What You Wished For

'New poetry at its
sparkling, thrilling best.'
Julia Bell

'Life affirming.'
Catherine Smith

n e w w r i t i n g . n e t